Cooking a Good Life Meal For Your Children

The Story of Jephthah

By

Daniel Phillips

All scripture verses are from the
KJV Version of the Bible

This book was printed in the United States of America.
Photo Credit: Beth Marie Photography, Owasso, OKlahoma

To order additional copies of this book contact:
Lion's Den Ministry
1190 North Mingo Road
Tulsa, OK   74116
Or
www.amazon.com

FWB

Table of Contents

Daniel Phillips is the pastor of the Airport Free Will Baptist Church in Tulsa, Oklahoma. He has been pastoring since 1977.

In the fall of 1989, he became founder of Lion's Den Ministries, a ministry to the forgotten smaller churches.

You can reach him at the following address:
Lion's Den Ministry
1190 North Mingo Road
Tulsa, OK   74116

Acknowledgments

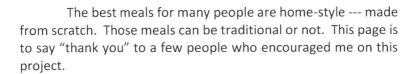

The best meals for many people are home-style --- made from scratch. Those meals can be traditional or not. This page is to say "thank you" to a few people who encouraged me on this project.

First, thanks to Wilma King who worked tirelessly on asking why I said this or that, and typing. My heart is full of pride to have her for a secretary.

Next, I want to say "thank you" to my children, Josh, Adam, Ben and Nathan. They are the delight of my heart! They have turned out to be fine young men and my prayer is that they will experience what I have --- love of family!

Lastly, I want to say "thank you" to my wife, Wanda, who for 38 years has helped me cook meaningful life meals when I was cooking poorly.

She is the great Ba-ya-day Chef in the family (Hebrew word for concern). Her cooking is always using the finest ingredients of tenderness and love.

Introduction
Culinary Courage

Most people are afraid to try new foods. Every region, country and culture has its own take on food. Are you willing to try ant eggs in Mexico or fried pickles in Arkansas? It would take a lot for me try rattlesnake! I know people say that it tastes like chicken, and that is the point. I will eat chicken but I don't want to eat rattlesnake. It isn't that I'm not adventuresome --- I just prefer the meat and potatoes theme, not snake and potatoes.

The average person probably is willing to try a new dish, but we all tend to gravitate towards what we like. Favorite foods become our comfort. It satisfies the need of not being intimidated. Life has so many things that are intimidating and as such we will shy away. Gourmet sounds intimidating and then we try some gourmet dish and our taste buds scream out, "You paid how much for this?"

This book is written to help you realize that just as each region and country has its definition of gourmet, so it is with the family function. The basis of this work is to examine a man named "Jephthah" and how he ate his own cooking. At the end of the day, he is not an expert on how to help his daughter, but he shows how to destroy life based on cooking stupid. To use the word stupid in this work is not meant to be condescending. It is used only to point out to the reader that anyone can cook a poor life meal for their family.

You will find in each devotional thought that we will examine four issues from a gourmet concept. Jephthah cooked a poor life meal because he was a bad chef. Next, J.D. (Jephthah's daughter) was able to take a poor life meal from her dad and cook her personal life meal with grace. Then a point is made about a recipe for overcoming Jephthah's foolish life meal by cooking life meals from God's cookbook, the <u>Bible</u>. The last point is how to cook a life meal that addresses the practical side. This has been done by creating a fictional chef's name, Chef Bayaday. This word is the Hebrew word for concern found in Psalms 138:8. In this writing, he is portrayed as a master chef who cooks good life meals as a parent.

The gourmet experts encourage us all to try new dishes, claiming them to be enjoyable, fun and delicious. They want us to reach for a new expanded culinary repertoire. Jephthah made up his own recipe and family relations. Today many fathers, mothers and grandparents are feeding their children dishes that are poor life meals of lessness. As such they are taking a good word and adding lessness. Meaning becomes meaninglessness, a continual state of no meaning. Children today by divorce, rejection, dysfunctional family dynamics, and a host of other negative experiences, sometimes have meals of meaninglessness. There is no created purpose or meaning in the life of the children.

Taking my cue from "The Beaver" on <u>Leave It To Beaver</u>, I make up words that are not grammatically correct. In one show of <u>Leave It To Beaver</u> his classmate was told by the teacher, "You know that is not a word," and Beaver's friend says, "If you can spell it, it is a word."

May these devotional thoughts help the parents to see how easy it is to create meals that are harmful to the soul, mind and emotional make-up. As a parent, learn to cook dishes that build up and not destroy your child.

It would be helpful to read Judges Chapter 11, which tells the story of how one man cooked a meal with deadly results for his daughter. There is a chapter called "The Story" that shares Judges Chapter 11. This chapter is written in my own words. As a parent, have the courage to be a culinary expert on how to nourish your children and grandchildren's lives. Nourish them with purpose so that you do not kill their spirit.

Lastly, you will notice a name, "Owen." He is my prayer partner and over 700 times he has met with me for prayer. While talking over a cup of coffee, he has become a positive muse for me, and I am honored by his prayers and encouragement.

Savoring

The concept of smart cooking for parents or grandparents is to provide good life meals. They should provide meals that nourish the soul into joie de vivre. Joie de vivre is a feeling of healthy enjoyment in life, or nourishing life meals.

To create meals that cause one to delight in the food is satisfying. The experience of good tasting food becomes a matter of "deep joy, of assured security, of living in the presence of God" (Sharing Food, 143). Joy is created by being able to savor food and by savoring a good life meal. Paul says that assured security is *"Whether therefore ye eat, or drink, or whatsoever ye do, do all to the glory of God."* (I Cor. 11:31)

Eating addresses the issues of life. Nourishment enables one to live. Malnourishment brings death. Parents want their children to be fed food that helps them grow. The truth be told, to nourish your child's soul takes more effort than fixing just a meal. Creating a life meal that enhances children in a positive way is hard work! Creating life meals that your children will savor is very difficult.

The role of a parent is to guide their child so that they can make good life choices --- to turn ingratitude into gratitude. Allow your sons and daughters to begin fixing healthy life meals that maintain enjoyment.

Jephthah's daughter (now called J. D.) was able to take a bad life meal and turn it into positive moments. She was better at cooking a good life meal than Jephthah. With dignity she turned her meaningless life meal into purpose. In the worthlessness of Jephthah's life meal she found worth. Today, America needs parents that can, want to, and will have the courage to cook life meals that build up and not tear down.

Savoring --- the smells, the taste, the decor, together with family and friends, makes a life meal that is enjoyable. Do you as a parent try to cook great life meals that nourish the heart of your children?

This book will show Jephthah's poor life meals, then J. D. cooking life meals with meaning and purpose.

The Story
Judges 11:1-11, 30-40

This story should be read from the Bible. What follows is my interpretation of the story.

As a mighty man of courage, Jephthah controlled much. What he could not control was what his family felt toward him. They had cast him out of the family because his mother was a harlot. Because of this he was not allowed to inherit anything from his father.

With great feeling of abandonment Jephthah left those who rejected him. Leaving his home town he settled in Tob. There he surrounded himself with a group of worthless men. During this time there was the threat of war.

Ammon and his people became aggressive toward Gilead. This aggression led the elders of Gilead to seek out Jephthah. He was a fighting man with a band of men ready to fight. They needed a leader!

So when the elders asked Jephthah to defend them, he asked "Why?" Jephthah told them that at one time they hated him and drove him away. Now they needed his help because they felt the distress of war.

The elders even agreed that if Jephthah took the job of going to war and won they would make him their leader. They even declared that the Lord witnessed this exchange making it a binding agreement.

It is after this agreement that the Spirit of the Lord moved on him. Full of a zeal for God and fueled with a desire to win, he made a vow. He vowed to offer as a burnt offering the first thing he saw when he returned home.

In the course of time Jephthah won and upon returning home he was met by his daughter. This moment brought him very low with sadness because he had made a vow. That burnt offering would now be his daughter!

Upon hearing what her father had done, Jephthah's daughter agreed to the vow. Asking for two months, she and her friends walked the mountain and mourned her unfulfilled womanhood. In the end she returned to him and willingly allowed him to sacrifice her. The story ends by saying he lived for six more years and then died.

An Important Note

The story of Jephthah is a story of strong emotional feelings. Basically there are two schools of thought. He either offers her as a real burnt sacrifice or he offers her up to serve the Lord and never have children.

An argument against him sacrificing his daughter says that no priest would do this, nor would the people allow it. Jeremiah does tell of a time when Israel offered up their sons and daughters as sacrifice (Jeremiah 7:31). The place is called Tophet and it is where Israel tried to get God's favor by offering up their sons and daughters. Israel in her misguided devotion polluted the land as well as their souls.

Also, why is Jephthah in the book of Hebrews? Chapter eleven is the faith chapter and you can find him listed with Sampson and Gideon. No one would ever say that these men did not have problems in their thoughts and actions. Yet they are part of the roll call of faith. These men were warriors. Believing in God, by faith, during times of war is what they were known for. One would never claim that these men were great examples of holiness.

The purpose of this book is not to debate whether or not he actually sacrificed his daughter. There are arguments on both sides. It is safe to say that he did violate a sacred trust. Dads need to guide and protect their children.

These concepts are given here, not for deeper debate but only to show a simple answer to a dark story.

A Recipe for Doing Stupid - Meaninglessness

Life has moments that are transforming--lying on your back watching the clouds, seeing leaves fall, hearing the flow of water flowing over rocks, or smelling the aroma of food that causes the mouth to water. These transforming moments are created by the right blends of ingredients.

Today the main criterion for food seems to be "fast and fresh." A good cook knows how to slice and dice the vegetables. A great cook has a longing to cook and to care for their guests. Such is the heart of the best cooks.

Cooking is a personal preference but it is given also by a personal performance. The creation is for all to enjoy. My aunt always created strange dishes such as can-can bread. The bread was baked in a coffee can and the sides of the bread were over cooked and the middle a little doughy. My mother always cooked with little regards to a recipe just adding a pinch of this, and a dash of that. However, they both created simple, memorable meals.

In the story of Jephthah one senses the recipe for devotion was forgotten. If you disregard the recipe your "vow" may come to be meaningless --- a dash of unclear thought or with a pinch of rashness which makes a bad tasting meal.

Cooking requires some thought and care. The best meals are made with the best ingredients carefully mixed and cooked together. Spam (known as the pig that flunked its physical) may be acceptable to the palate but two meals of it may be too much.

The meals that one savors are the ones that create meaning, making us long for a meal with good conversation.

Jephthah "cooked his own goose" because his recipe for life never created a Bon Appétit with good conversation. He seasoned his goose with meaninglessness--a continual state of having no meaning. If his vow had good meaning then his dish of sacrifice would have had seconds. Others would have wanted to follow his recipe. "'No one asked for seconds, not even Jephthah," says Owen.

Jephthah is the quintessential cook that reveals much of how people cook their own life difficulties. Today ask yourself if you are creating a meaningful dish for your family, friends, co-workers, or for yourself. Watch out for your meaningless actions that create meaninglessness. Gene Kissinger always says, "mighty tasty" to a good meal. Remember meaningless actions are never tasty.

Cooking with J.D.

J. D. was a special and rare individual --- she cooked her life meal with meaning. She was a better daughter than Jephthah was a father. Her life ended with a degree of meaning and purpose. As a young lady she was able to maintain her individuality in the social context of a male dominated society. Her obedience is remarkable -- NO, very remarkable. She could easily inspire a Proverbs 32 daughter that would follow the Proverbs 31 woman.

That obedience reveals a character of fixed direction. Judges 11 is silent on many fronts (the western mind wants more detail) but she steadfastly expresses her role as a daughter. Her life meal of obedience allows for over 3100 years of people remembering her. Shakespeare asked, "What's in a name?" The name J. D. stands for all young ladies who cook life meals with meaning. Meaning for her was obedience even in the face of abnormal behavior.

God's Recipe for Overcoming Meaninglessness

Remember: Meaninglessness is a continual state of no meaning.

* **Take two cups of Proverbs 3:5-6:**
    (5) "Trust in the Lord with all thine heart; and lean not unto thine own understanding."
    (6) "In all thy ways acknowledge Him, and He shall direct thy paths."

* **Mix in one cup of firm Principle:**
    (Daniel 1:8) *"But Daniel purposed in his heart that he would not defile himself with ...."*

* **Mix well - meditate every hour for 24 hours Psalms 1:2:**
    - *"But his delight is in the law of the Lord; and in his law doth he mediate day & night."*

* **After 24 hours of meditation:**
    - Add a pinch of Keeping the word (Revelations 3:10).
    - Add a spoonful of Acts 2:42a, *"and they continued steadfastly."*

* **Stir in two cups of obedience:**
    - (I Peter 1:22) *"Seeing ye have purified your souls in obeying the truth through the Spirit, unto unfeigned love of the brethren, see that ye love one another with a pure heart fervently."*

Owen says, "A good life meal from the Bible has lasting results on kids."

Becoming a Bayaday Chef

Psalms 138:8 says, *"The Lord will perfect that which concerneth me."* The Hebrew word for concern is pronounced Ba-ya-day. The Lord's concern for you is the same concern that a parent should have for their children, thus becoming a Bayaday parent.

Parents who want to become a Master Chef or an Iron Chef have to show concern--concern for the type of life meal one cooks.

Everyone has heard the phrase "Bon Appétit" or good appetite. Enjoying the meal is what great chefs want. One can also experience Marvais Appétit or bad food or a bad meal. No one would say Jephthah's vow was a Bon Appétit or a joyful experience.

If you want to be a Bayaday Chef you have to realize the joy in nourishing family with great life meals. What is the long term benefit of the life meal you cook today?

Menus that Matter

To be a Master Chef like Chef Bayaday you need to have menus that produce Bon Appétit of meaning. One of the best ways to create meaning and meaningful life meals is by creating traditions. Chef Bayaday says that Christmas tree ornaments are a great start. Each year every child gets their own tree ornament. When they grow up and leave home they receive a box full of their tree ornaments.

What is even greater is to do this with the grandchildren. The tradition that is created is able to tie the past Christmases with the present Christmases. Over time the experience becomes a great life meal of meaning or Bon Appétit.

My Menus For Life Meals of Bon Appétit

1. Write you own menu of Bon Appétit.

2. Write you own menu of a Life Meal of Meaning.

A Recipe for Doing Stupid - Worthlessness

Jephthah's story reveals that the central component to life is not religious zeal, but living life by sustaining a good relationship with God. Notwithstanding, the difficulties at the most basic level is that the vow seems to exist more from a secular world view. There is very little thought for a Deuteronomy world view which is an acceptance of God's rule in life. Men of power may not be men of character. Jephthah's story can be examined from the standpoint of interpersonal relations that one has with family and God. Preachers can minster effectively to their members but fail in their relationships with family. Sometimes a family suffers by one's devotion.

The popular dynamic of Jephthah's day may accept offering up your children, but it was never God's way. The book of Judges, chapter 11, tells the story that shows the results of living by one's own code of cooking. Israel has been influenced time and time again by other nations allowing them to be "Canaanized in their character," states Daniel Block. It is a frightening thing to be affected in your character so that you are willing to act with abnormal behavior. If you are what you eat, then truly you are what your character becomes.

Gail Townsend says the story leaves one cold and alone. Wanda Phillips proclaims, "It is selfish to have a self-seeking vow." Gary LaBass believes Jephthah's story points to many today -- those who are carried away by their own desires (James 4:1-3).

This is a man of valor, but he loses the great battle for family. Why? He is carried away from common sense with an overcoming sense for power. And, Ron Palmer says, "A misguided, self-willed desire to worship according to the flesh and not the Spirit." This attitude for power allows one to drift into "lessness" of personality, or as Owen says, "A bad decision maker."

Jephthah displaced his daughter's life by breaking the sacred bond a father should have which is to "protect the family." His vow devalued his life and destroyed his daughter. One wonders if she wanted to say "Et tu Brute" -- an act of treachery by someone close.

Jephthah's vow is authentic to him. It's like making a tomato sauce when wearing a white shirt. If not careful the stain will ruin it, so it becomes worthless. Jephthah's vow shows the worthlessness of his cooking a life meal. His meal stained his soul! He was brought "very low," or "very sad" (v.35). His dish of the day became his worthlessness for the remaining 2,250 days of his life -- 2,250 days of worthlessness and sadness.

Be very careful as a dad or mom so that you don't cook six years and two months of worthlessness!

Cooking with J. D.

When it comes to Jephthah, his cookbook does not sell. Who wants a dish of the day of worthlessness? J. D. is an executive chef that is cooking a life meal. Did you ever feel the icy hand of abandonment? Alone, forsaken, and no help coming, are powerful feelings. J. D. had to eat a life meal of her father's choice.

Jephthah's life meal was, "I will abandon you to fulfill my desire." J. D.'s life meal became a meal of value. She valued the integrity of her purity.

Years later Malachi wrote about God's desire to counter parents like Jephthah:

"and he shall turn the hearts of the fathers to the children ..." (3:6).

Malachi 3:5-6 is as enigmatic as Judges 11--the perplexing issue of a dysfunctional family relating to who is cooking poor life meals.

No relationship is worthless if reconciliation happens. J. D. shows this reconciliation by saying, *"Do to me according to that which hath proceeded out of thy mouth"* (Judges 11:36). There is a natural tone to J.D.'s words, whereas mine would probably be hateful. She maintains her acceptance of her father, and this is her worth.

God's recipe for Overcoming Worthlessness

Remember: Worthlessness is a continual state of feeling no worth.

* **Take a cup of John 3:16 (the value God places on you):**
"For God so loved (me) the world that he gave his only begotten Son, that whosoever believeth on him should not perish, but have everlasting life."

* **Take a cup of Mattthew 5:44 (love your enemies) with a cup of John 13:34 (love one another):**
These cups are the value you place on people.

* **Take a cup of Leviticus 19:18, Mathew 19:19 (*love they neighbor as thyself*):**
This is the value you place on yourself in Christ.

Owen says, "God is great at putting good in people so that they can do good."

Becoming a Bayaday Chef

Psalms 138:8 tells us that God is concerned about us. You as a parent engage God's attention. He really is interested about your becoming a Bayaday Chef with the understanding of du jour. Du jour means the dish of the day.

Have you ever gone to a Dinner Theater -- a drama and a meal? Jephthah became the executive chef of his dinner theater. His dish of the day was based on his own absorbed self-will. Chef Bayaday says he knows a lot of men as the executive chef of their family, who are cooking worthless life meals.

Menus That Matter

Chef Bayaday has a friend that cooks a great life meal based on a principle. The principle is to help children to learn about why families sacrifice.

The family would plan their vacation. In doing so they talked about how they would save. They sacrificed and saved to enjoy a better vacation later. As the years pass the children begin to give. Those times add great worth to the family. This is the du jour of life--life with worth or purpose.

My Menus for Life Meals of Du jour

1. My own menu for the Dish of the Day.

2. My own menu for worth.

A Recipe for Doing Stupid - Kindlessness

When I was growing up I would sometimes hear "that will do" which was a statement for "that's enough!" It was enough hours of playing or maybe enough working for the day.

The phrase, "that will do" is really a God concept. When God created the world He stated, "It is good" which means well pleasing or proper. His statement is much like "that will do." When God was creating, He saw that it was good so that each aspect of His handiwork is declared good. That good is added to by the phrase *"after their kind"* (Genesis 1:21), which is good being sustainable. Sustainability allows for continuity whether physical or spiritual. The sustainability of how one relates to God is the story of the Bible. Remember, Elijah had his Elisha which allowed religious authority to pass from one generation to another-- "after its kind." Elisha had Gehazi, but because Gehazi sinned, Israel lost the sustainability of great prophets.

During the time of Judges, Israel failed to maintain sustainability. Society ebbed towards perishing because Israel did not try to sustain their covenant relationship with God. Sustainability was lost when Israel would "forsake the Lord" to do "evil in the sight of the Lord". The Kirbmister, David "R" Kirby says, "When people do what they want, then they usually do what God doesn't want." Owen Austin says, "Men want to live godless more than being godly."

Within a patchwork of characters, called Judges, some sustain their life with a sweet relationship towards God. Yet, some of the judges did not. Judges, as a whole, could be a cookbook -- or recipes for foolish actions.

Jephthah's story is a recipe of how to cook a bitter dish. It is not even a bittersweet dish. It is very bad tasting, bitter and bordering on the verge of making one physically ill. After reading about Jephthah one wants to wash their hands much like Pilate did at Jesus' trial.

How is sweetness in life truly experienced? By kindness! Kindness is being polite, friendly and encouraging towards people.

Jephthah does not have kindness because he lacks any real thought on how to have a sweet life. To him his sweet life would be acceptance from those who had rejected him.

Cooking with J.D.

J. D. as a young cook seemingly understood her life meal had to maintain kindness. She took her father's life meal (he thought it was a sweet thing to make a vow) which was negative and made it positive.

Did you ever hear about the argument to eat desserts? You can't eat pork because of swine flu and you can't eat chicken because of bird flu. You can't eat beef because of mad cow disease and you can't eat eggs because of salmonella. You can't eat fish because heavy metal poison is in the water. And, you can't eat fruits and vegetables because of the insecticides and herbicides. Hummmmmm!!! I believe that leaves chocolate and ice cream! Remember "stressed" spelled backward is desserts (Gusher, September 2012). In her stress J. D. makes a positive dessert.

As J. D. sees her father returning from battle she runs out to meet him. She is gifted in the use of timbrels and dance, and as her father returns she expresses her joy and thankfulness with music and dance.

It is here that Jephthah has walked into his Marah (Exodus 15:23) -- the place of bitterness, a place of no sweet life. When people experience kindness, it shows on their face. Here Jephthah's thrill is gone! Here it dawns on him that he will miss these moments of astonishment with his grandchildren. J. D. comes with a smile to meet her father. Then she has to eat his poorly cooked life meal. In cooking her life meal she cooks it by being remembered as the young girl that showed her father a kindness that costs her. She had to eat his vow.

God's recipe for Overcoming Kindlessness

Remember: Kindlessness is a continual state of showing no kindness.

* **Take one cup of understanding:**
    Life is not perfect; therefore, it is hard to get a cup of understanding. Good understanding takes clear thinking.
* **Take one cup of willingness to make significant life changes:**
    This is an insurmountable obstacle for some.
* **Mix both cups together and add:**
    The water of life - Jesus (John 4:13-14).
* **Next add a tablespoon of desire:**
    Proverbs 19:22 - *"The desire of a man is his kindness"*. This kindness has to be from a heart that has not been made bitter by rejection.

Bake by prayer:
    To create a life meal that is sweet takes kindness. Moses experienced the bitter waters at Marah. Bitterness from rejection makes life's meal bitter beyond endurance. Handle your bitterness and exchange it for kindness in your heart.

"You become old when you fail to be astonished by Jesus. Astonish your children by a good life meal." says Owen.

Becoming a Bayaday Chef

When children's lives are full of bitterness there is a loss of kindness. The Italian word "Dolce Vita" or "sweetness in life" is missing. It means a point where food and life's experiences satisfy.

To be a Bayaday Chef that can cook life meals that are Dolce Vita takes a heart that wants to show kindness toward one's children. This is the heart of Psalms 138:8-- God's concern for us in time of trouble. Such concern is kindness in life.

Menus that Matter

Chef Bayaday tells of a young father who was doing Colossians 3:21 which says *"provoke not your children to anger".* Instead of not provoking, he provoked. Young children can feel a loss of sweetness in life by being told they are never good enough or have no value. From sports, school or any activity, parents can and do bully. Being bullied takes the sweetness out of life.

To be a successful chef or to become a Bayaday Chef one has to show kindness or Dolce Vita. Be very careful about exasperating your children. Start over when you realize you are provoking your children unto anger. Sit down and say, "I'm sorry." Teach that kindness is a learned experience.

My Menus for Life Meals for Dolce Vita

1. My own menu for Dolce Vita.

2. My own menu for kindness. Be careful that you don't use money or things to replace kindness.

A Recipe for Doing Stupid – Aimlessness

Did you ever do something and then say to yourself - "Why did I do that?" The answer is, "Boy that was stupid!" "Stupid is, as stupid does", states the movie character philosophy of Forrest Gump.

One of the easiest ways to do stupid things is to jump to the wrong conclusions. The other day a man in a truck honked at me and pointed down. I said to myself, "What is his problem?" Ten minutes later I realized that he was trying to warn me that my tire was going flat. But all I could think of was, "What is his problem?"

Jumping to the wrong conclusion is easy -- usually causing misunderstanding or a stupid action. Jephthah used the ingredient of aimless thinking and jumped to the wrong conclusion. Since I jumped to the wrong conclusion when the man honked at me, I robbed myself of peace.

The author of Jephthah's story leads us to understand why Jephthah made an aimless vow. He is a Gileadite, a great warrior. He is shamed by his father for being born of a harlot. His step-brother rejects him and even Gilead rejects him. There is no inheritance and he becomes the leader of a group of worthless men.

The children of Ammon (v.4) make war with Israel and the elders want Jephthah to become their general/leader. If he is victorious he will be the governor over Gilead (v.9) and, the elders agree to this (v.11).

It is because he eats aimlessness. In having no good aim in life, he feels the need to have a vow (v.30) that becomes his main dish. He creates a dish that should not have been cooked. He uses the ingredients of aimlessness. Out of a heart of rejection he is aimless in his vow. Jephthah shows how modern men can be aimless in their purpose of life by reaching the wrong conclusion.

Cooking with J.D.

Aimlessness in preparing a life meal does not stimulate the appetite. Jephthah should have been more careful with his aimless vow. What he did was to create a negative life meal.

To create a meal that causes one to delight in eating can be satisfying. L. Shannon Jung says, "good food becomes a matter of deep joy, of assured security, of being in the presence of God". (Sharing Food.145). Jephthah does not do any of this.

Deep joy comes from the ability to savor good food. Savory is the meaningful experiences in life and as such should be an aim in our lives. The assured security Jung speaks of is expressed by Paul, *"Whether therefore ye eat, or drink, or whatsoever ye do, do all to the glory of God"* (I Corinthians 10:31).

Eating addresses the issues of life. Satisfying meals nourish our lives. But to truly live life you have to nourish the emotional and mental parts of life. Talk to a child and ask them about an important day that they remember. What day did J. D. remember? Were there days of joy and happiness in her life? Probably, but the end of her father's life meal was aimless yet hers had value.

When it comes to J. D., she can only savor her one great asset which was her purity! She overcame the aimlessness of her father's meal by knowing what was important to her. She savored her purity!

God's Recipe for Overcoming Aimlessness

Remember: Aimlessness is a continual state of having no aim or purpose.

* **Take two cups of good purpose** (Daniel 1:8) and add:
* **One tablespoon of** *"commit thy way unto the Lord"* by doing Proverbs 3:5-6.
* **Next, stir in ½ cup of Proverbs 15:8b**, *"the prayer of the upright is his delight."*
* **Mix in Jeremiah 29:13**, *"And ye shall seek me, and find me, when ye shall search for me with all your heart."*
* **Last, add two cups of Psalms 37:4-5**, *"Delight thyself also in the Lord; and he shall give thee the desires of thine heart. Commit thy way unto the Lord; trust also in him; and he shall bring it to pass."*

Owen says, "I found my purpose in experiencing God's grace and my aim is to try and give it away."

Becoming a Bayaday Chef

There is a big difference between Judges 11:1-2 and Psalms 138:8. Judges expresses the root of Jephthah's problem, whereas Psalms 138:8 expresses God's aim, intention or goal for us. Judges 11:1-2 is Jephthah's hors d'oeuvre -- literally a small bite-sized food to stimulate one's appetite before the main course. His main dish was his vow (11:30-31), but his hors d'oeuvre was rejection.

Parenting to some degree is much like a shot in the dark or a purposeless aim. When a parent's judgment violates Psalms 138:8 then one misses the aim of cooking positive life meals.

Menus that Matter

Chef Bayaday tells of a young couple who tried to make birthdays more meaningful by putting a lot of thought into planning the party. The party is the main dish but getting ready is the hors d'oeuvre. It takes energy to nourish the heart and emotions! One little girl, as she watched her parents get things ready for her birthday said, "This is a happy day!" She is savoring a moment that nourishes her soul.

My Menus for Life Meals of Hors D'oeuvre

1. My own menu for hors d'oeuvre.

2. My own menu for aiming at a goal.

A Recipe for Doing Stupid – Cluelessness

Like a ship that needs a compass to maintain its bearing through overpowering weather, so must a man have direction to keep him on the right course. Living in today's world has changed the concept of what keeps the soul on the right path. Some see Jesus as keeping the soul on course and others do not. Some reject the dogma of the church and truth becomes what you believe.

Jephthah shows how a man had no objective truth when it came to people. In his state of cluelessness, he misunderstands truth.

I remember a *Bugs Bunny* show where Yosemite Sam, who is the royal cook, takes a meal to the king. The king said, "It's the same thing day after day. I want Hasenpfeffer!" Yosemite Sam has looked the word up, and, voila, Hasenpfeffer is "rabbit." The heart of the show is how Yosemite Sam tries to snare Bugs. True to style, Bugs becomes the cook, Sam is placed in prison and the king declares, "Cook, where is my dinner?" True to form, Bugs brings him a dish and the king says as he eats, "If I didn't know that this was Hasenpfeffer I would swear that it was carrots." Bugs replies, "A one eyed Jack can always beat a king." This shows a new truth that is a wrong truth.

Jephthah is eating carrots when he thinks he is eating Hasenpfeffer (peppered rabbit). Jephthah's Hasenpfeffer is that he thinks he is pious, but the truth is that "he is not pious (in the Orthodox Yahwistic sense). He was outright pagan." (The New American Commentary, 367)

It seems that Jephthah had a duel relationship with spiritual reality. On the one hand he is Canonized (acted like the nations around him), but he wanted God's blessing. When one no longer sees the validity of truth but mixes different competing ideas, he finds himself in a constant state of being clueless.

In Bugs Bunny, the king believed he was going to have a great meal of Hasenpfeffer but it was carrots. The Prodigal Son of Luke 15 rejects his father's truth-- living effectively in God's will. The Son found that wasting his father's truth did not satisfy. It was "hog food" or carrots instead of Hasenpfeffer.

Jephthah's reality was sadness and he probably was clueless in how to live in God's will and change the vow.

Cooking with J.D.

The fictional character, Sherlock Holmes, said, "Come Watson, the game is afoot." Then off they would go looking for clues. Judges 11:1 is a clue for much that happened in J.D.'s life. Her father's desire to be accepted affected her life meal and life. The reason was her father is clueless as to how to handle his own soul.

Rejection has been his life meal for a long time. He didn't have help in overcoming this negative personality trait. Proverbs 11:17a gives an insightful look into life--*"A merciful man doeth good to his own soul."*

The cluelessness of his life kept him from nourishing his own soul. Here is the ethical struggle of human personality. How do you nourish yourself but also others with positive life meals? Proverbs 11:17b says, *"A cruel man brings trouble on himself."* Healthy minds, hearts or souls happen out of acts of mercy toward others. Here mercy is revealed in acceptance of her father's desire. She did not rebel but experiences an inner perspective that allows mercy to forgive. The passage does not say that she forgave, but one can sense that to accept she would have to forgive.

Jephthah's life meal for J.D. was cruel. J.D. was not cruel but in mercy she would do well to her soul.

God's Recipe for Overcoming Cluelessness:

Remember: Cluelessness is a continual state of not knowing how to cook a meaningful life meal.

* Take one cup of a multitude of mercy:

(Psalms 5:7) *"But as for me I will come into thy house in the multitude of mercy ..."*

Multitude of mercy means increase -- refers to the abundance of God's mercies.

* Add two cups of mercy for distress:

(Psalms 4:1) *"Hear me when I call, O God ... thou hast enlarged me when I was in distress ...say that his mercy endureth forever."*

(Psalms 118:4c-5a) *"I called upon the Lord in distress."*

* Stir in a tablespoon of mercy:

(Psalms 90:14) *"Oh satisfy us early with thy mercy that we may rejoice and be glad all our days."*

* Add one-half cup of trusted mercy and song:

(Psalms 13:5) *"But I have trusted in thy mercy, my heart shall rejoice in thy salvation."*

(Psalms 13:6) *"I will sing unto the Lord because he hath dealt bountifully with me."*

It is good to eat once a day an awareness of God's mercy, knowing that God's mercy keeps cluelessness away.

Owen says; "Handle your own rejection without involving your children".

Becoming a Bayaday Chef

Sometimes as a parent one can be clueless about what they should do. Broken families have many clueless times. These good life meals can aid the hurting and confused child of broken homes or divorce.

When one finds himself in a broken or divorced home the parent needs to realize that life meals may not be positive. But, to be constructive it is necessary to do some "picking up" after something has been dissolved. Children may wake up one day eating carrots when they think they are dining on Hasenpfeffer.

The parent who wants to be a Bayaday Chef, even though they are divorced or single, must rely not on a child or children to meet an emotional and acceptance issue. The child or children may have witnessed the hurt to a point where they become emotional and begin to feel abandonment. Psalms 138:8 is a way to help children to move beyond their own shattered life.

Menus that Matter

Chef Bayaday says he knows of a divorced couple and what seems to be helpful in the emotional hurts is a "Forgiveness Tree." The concept is that it is never easy to forgive. When one has those negative feelings and anger, just write down how you feel on a piece of paper. Nail it to the "Forgiveness Tree". Help the children to realize that this is what Jesus did in Luke 23:24.

My Menus for Life Meals of Having a Clue

1. My own menu for creating a life meal that gives a clue of how to live life well.

2. My own menu for creating a life meal that shows the difference between carrots and Hasenpfeffer.

A Recipe for Doing Stupid – Tastelessness

Pâté in cooking is a spread used to go with hors d'oeuvres. The spread is made as a paste much like potted meat. The pâté is made out of vegetables, fruits, or meats that are finely chopped.

One can develop a liking for some foods. The taste is very agreeable to the experience of eating. Jephthah made his own Pâté and you have to ask, "How did that taste?"

The home recipe Jephthah used was not the one that was approved by Jehovah (Deuteronomy 12:31). He created a *tasteless* pâté in an effort to create a *tasteful* pâté. He evidently did not read Jehovah's recipe book. With mental dullness he was foolish to eat his own Pâté.

If you are going to make a pâté for family and friends, don't be deceived into thinking that it will have a great taste. Jephthah's pâté was made from "proprio motu", which means a willingness to act by personal choice. By his own decision he made the wrong pâté.

To choose to make one's pâté by rejecting the "God Recipe" book (Deuteronomy) leads to tastelessness. Some people find olives tasteless, and some find mushrooms tasteless so they never eat them. Today, if you watch some of the cooking shows on television when dealing with mushrooms some say, "they are earthy," meaning tasting or smelling like earth. Earthy also means worldly.

It is easy to become at ease in clear thinking. Jephthah wanted so much to be accepted by winning the war that his vow became tasteless. The dish was tasteless because it became earthy--pertaining to the earth as opposed to heavenly.

Jephthah was earthbound in his thinking. He was lacking sophistication in the reading of God's recipe book, which would have created a pâté of heavenly taste.

Cooking with J. D.

How is it that something as beautiful as life can become a tragedy? Jephthah and J. D.'s story is like a Greek tragedy. Had Jephthah flabbergasted his family before? Had they always suffered with his self-centered, tasteless demands? It almost seems that he is uncaring and devoid of any redeeming love.

He is a man of great conviction by not going back on his vow. Maybe he never realized that this was wrong thinking! Did he ever have doubts about his action? His life meal for J. D. was tasteless!

What would he write on the gravestone? "J. D., daughter of a tasteless man?" His pate' is worse than potted meat!

J. D. on the other hand had the grace of a dancer. She had a heart for joyful dance which is a zest to enjoy life. What goes on in the mind of a dancer? Can she hear her own music and dance to it? She comes with "timbrels" and "dances". The acoustical quality of the timbrel gives it an independent sound allowing for dance. With rhythmical dance she leaps and skips a dance of victory.

Jephthah's pate' was a tasteless life's meal. J. D.'s pate' was a life of dance!

God's Recipe for Overcoming Tastelessness

Remember: Tastelessness is a continual state of cooking a life meal and not allowing for choice.

* **Take three cups of liquid --- "rejoicing the heart."**
    (Psalms 19:8) *"The statutes of the Lord are right, rejoicing the heart ..."*

* **Mix two cups of "oil of joy."**
    (Isaiah 61:3) *"give them ... oil of joy for mourning."*

* **Next slowly stir in ½ cup of the sweetener of empowering joy:**
    (Nehemiah 8:10c) *"for the joy of the Lord is your strength."*

This drink helps to refresh, relax, restart, and revive your spirit. This enables one to keep on going and to keep on dancing.

Owen says, "If the work of the Lord excites you, you will find zest!"

Becoming a Bayaday Chef

"The Lord will perfect that which concerneth me" says Psalms 138:8. The Lord relates to a person's affairs. The great chefs know that to make a pâté can be frustrating. The wrong ingredients or a poor quality can destroy a pâté. The same is true about life and its inconsistency. Lack of energy, money, or even time can erode one's perception. Jephthah believed he was doing well for his family but created a pâté of sadness.

Can a parent ever get it right? Parenting is hard and demanding! Chef Bayaday says that a great tasting pâté would be a mix of consistency and simple. To be inconsistent in actions and discipline creates a family in chaos. The failure to have simple moments in a life meal can lead to times of confusion. Being consistent sets the boundaries, and simple allows for one to depressurize life.

Menus that Matter

Chef Bayaday knows of a couple who helped their children to understand the idea of simple and consistent, to set goals and depressurize life. Talk to your children and ask them to name what they believe to be simple goals for a life meal. When goals have been established ask them to tell the story of Jephthah in their own words.

The telling of the story allows the children to understand what the acceptable behavior becomes. It is the acceptable behavior that becomes one's pâté. This will also keep parents from becoming loud and inconsistent. Did you ever hear a parent say, "You never do anything right!", or" Why can't you be more like your brother/sister?" as their voice rises higher. Having simple, consistent goals that children understand will make a great tasting pâté.

My Menu for Life Meals of Tastefulness

1. My own good tasting pâté that is consistent.

2. My own good tasting pâté that is simple.

A Recipe for Doing Stupid – Condimentlessness

There are four basic sensations the tongue can taste: sour, bitter, salty, and sweet. Pickles can be created with all four basic tastes. There is distinctive taste to the different types of pickles. The pickles can have a high bodied taste or a low bodied taste, depending on how long they are in the pickling solution. Pickles are never seen as "main dishes" of a meal, but only as condiments to enhance the meal or they can be eaten alone.

Jephthah, no doubt with a strong resolve, said, "I'll sacrifice and then no one will question my devotion to God." He knew that even Abraham's devotion was tied to his willingness to offer his son. Jephthah probably thought that since God had helped Abraham, He would help him.

Two months have passed. All is ready. The house is quiet. The question in Jephthah's mind is, "Will an angel show up?" What can he say? Today his voice is not full of strength and resolve. Now you can hear the doubt and confusion and the lack of resolve. He had drowned in his own self will. Society is drowning. His family is drowning. Every man is doing what is right in his own eyes (Judges 17:6), which is the ugly truth of self will. Could he find a priest to offer the sacrifice, or did he do it himself?

Lifting the knife, what prayer did he pray, or did his mind shout out to his soul, "You are in a pickle!" Those moments in life where you are experiencing troublesome, awkward, and intensely painful situations become your pickle. They are times when the condiments should enhance the meal, not destroy the meal! Today with knife in hand he has made a very bad tasting pickle that will cause him to taste the strong acid taste of bitterness and sadness.

How can a man create such a bad tasting condiment for life? First, one fails to have a clear recipe for pickle making. He fails to analyze his own thoughts. He approaches his life with an overwhelming sense of self-confidence. With a cocky attitude he becomes self-centered, looking only to his own interests. Being engrossed in self he could not see clearly, leading to self-deception. In deceiving himself he felt that his determination was justified. His self-determination in making the vow was acted upon by his own will.

He made this pickle for one reason. He was self-driven and chose a selfish behavior. People make their own pickles in life when it is all about self, which is the direct opposite of selflessness. Self-will brings sour and bitter pickles that ruin good meals. If you are going to eat pickles choose the right kind of pickle.

Cooking with J. D.

Jephthah's moment of being in a pickle caused his life meal to be sour. His rejection in life caused him to keep his life meal in the pickling solution too long.

This becomes his humbling moment. He believed his life meal would be a great experience and yet he found it was not. J. D. had to eat her father's pickled life meal. His humble pie made of pickles was not a humble pie of J.D.'s making.

Humble pie starts with the entrails of a deer. A meal is made from the least desirable parts of the deer. It is a meal given to the servants after a hunt. The term "humble pie" is understood to show humiliation by admitting one's error.

J. D.'s humble pie was not made because she had done something wrong. No, her humble pie is in relation to her spirit. She had a willingness to be a servant to her father's will. It was a desire to do her duty. She was not a doormat because she was meek. No, her integrity allowed her to serve her father.

Did you ever go to a restaurant to eat and receive poor service? The waiter failed to perform at an acceptable level. Poor service can diminish a good meal. J.D.'s life meal did not diminish her! Her father's life meal was bad tasting, sour pickles. J. D. turned her life meal into sweet pickles by serving Jephthah's wish.

God's Recipe for Overcoming Sour Pickles

Remember: Condimentlessness is a continual state of poor attitude when cooking a life meal.

* Take one cup of devotion to Christ:
(Ephesians 3:17) *"That Christ may dwell in your hearts by faith; that ye, being rooted and grounded in love."*

* Add three cups of multi-purpose sweetness:
Removes the sourness of a life meal by gruff men and critical women that need sweetness. Multi-purpose sweetness is:

1) (Revelation 1:18) *"Jesus is alive for everyone"* -- sweet life eternal.

2) (John 14:1) *"Let not your heart be troubled: ye believe in God, believe also in me"* -- trouble free sweetness.

3) (Luke 5:11) *"they forsook all and followed him."* -- sweet devotion.

* Cover and place in oven of rejoicing:
(Deuteronomy 26:11) *"And thou shalt rejoice in every good thing which the Lord hath given unto thee ....*

Life meals that are sour need the condiments of sweet eternal life, a trouble-free heart, and an attitude of sweet devotion.

Owen says, "Stay positive and sweet by being careful of the condiments you put on your life meal."

Becoming a Bayaday Chef

A Bayaday Chef is always one who looks for the practical with intentional results. This is the heart of Psalms 138:8. God is practical and intentional in dealing with us. If you want to cook a great life meal, do it by becoming practical and intentional in the use of condiments! Pickles can be a condiment the same as mustard or catsup. Just be sure they are the right kind of pickle!

History says that Cleopatra ate pickles for her beauty and spirituality. Julius Caesar thought that pickles were good for one's health. Jephthah found the type of condiments he used for his daughter's life meal was a very poor choice. His choice was never practical and had no intention to aid. Many parents fail their children in a practical life meal. Why? They have little to do with their children. They create moments where the children never feel good enough or smart enough. Chef Bayaday says that some always give sour pickles. After a while, one tires of that taste very quickly.

Menus that Matter

A good way to teach your children the importance of having the right condiments is to take a scoop of ice cream. Doctor it up by putting pickles, mustard and catsup on it. These are condiments that are suited for hamburgers, not ice cream. Teach children to be sure to choose good and right condiments for their life meal.

Parents can get five or six different types of pickles. Take one of each, allowing your children to experience the different tastes. Explain the difference and help the children to choose the taste that they desire for their life. Chef Bayaday says that parents can once a month have a "pickle day" which allows their children to express their moods about life.

My Menu for Life Meals of Using the Correct Condiments

1. My own choice of condiments which are practical for children are:

2. My own choice of condiments which are intentional for my children are:

A Recipe for Doing Stupid – Fruitlessness

Jephthah's desire was to have "haute cuisine," the high-end meal. High-end cooking may appeal to the eye but may not be as satisfying to the taste or filling. Bad tasting food or bad smelling food has fruitlessness to it. Why? Because the meal does not produce a benefit to the taste or smell. Fruitlessness with food is food that never satisfies the eater by taste or smell. Jephthah may have believed his vow would satisfy, but what he learned was that the meal both tasted and smelled badly, plus it was too expensive.

High-end cooking (haute cuisine) opens one up to new tastes and experiences. Such meals are seen as the "good life."

With the Spirit of the Lord upon him (11:29) Jephthah no doubt began to think about winning. He probably began to dream about winning, acceptance, and being the leader. Such dreams would enter his mind as his own life meal. He wanted a moment of feeling accepted by all. That would be his good life!

Everyone wants to be inspired or wants a good life. To get the "good life" or the "high-end" life, Jephthah becomes willing to make a vow.

Three thousand, four hundred and thirty years later, people still desire a fruitful life. Deuteronomy tells Israel about God's plan for the "haute cuisine." Because Jephthah did not understand the "haute cuisine" he experienced a bad life meal.

We have to wonder if Jephthah's sacrifice happened on Monday, and if so, whether he hated the Mondays of his life. In modern America only three percent see Mondays as their favorite day. This day would be his Monday—not a favorite day! His "haute cuisine" would leave his eyes joyless. His mind no doubt would dwell more on the negatives of life. This meal would surrender him to a cold heart, overwhelmed by fear and personal guilt.

Did other towns use his name in the jokes of the day? "Hey, Jephthah, your village called and they are missing the idiot." Did he ever fear what he would become without his daughter or grandchildren that complete the circle of love in life? Maybe he wonders what his life could have been, and yet tries not to succumb to guilt.

Jephthah misunderstood the "haute cuisine" because he was more interested in just his own good life. You become a Jephthah when your only concern for the "good life" is for yourself and not others. Such action is fruitlessness that causes you to pay for a meal that smells and tastes badly.

Cooking with J. D.

J. D.'s story should be required reading for all who want to bear fruit in their lives. The story gives pause, but also forces the reader to see attitudes and how attitudes affect one's life meal.

J. D. is able to take her father's haute cuisine (high-end meal), that was really a very poor life meal, and rework it. Jephthah's life meal was a fruitless meal with no great redeeming value. J. D. had 1,440 hours to live! With the clock ticking she made the most of those two months. No doubt, walking the hills of Gilead allowed her time to sharpen her devotion.

The benefits of those two months are not wasted. J. D. and her friends created a fruitful life meal, and her haute cuisine is remembrance. For the next 3,500 years people will remember her life meal in a positive way.

J. Carnegie (Bruce G. Weber, P. 39) says, "Grow nourishing food and you will become a valuable citizen." Thomas Jefferson, referring to farmers said, "The cultivators of the earth are the most valuable citizens." I say that parents who nourish their children by cultivating great life meals are the real heroes. Great life meals are wholesome and sustain the soul. They are not a malnourishing life meal like Jephthah's. J. D. is remembered because she nourishes her soul with purity and remains pure.

God's Recipe for Overcoming Fruitlessness

Remember: Fruitlessness is a constant state of having no good fruit in life.

* **Two cups of meditation fruit are:**
(Psalms 1:1) Clear counsel of the godly -- stay away from the fruit of the scornful.
(Psalms 119:16) -- Love for the Word. *"I will delight myself in thy statues: I will not forget thy word."*

* **Add the sweetener of one-half cup of conversion:**
(Psalms 19:7) A change of heart -- converting the soul.

* **Add three tablespoons of heavenly honey:**
God's word sweetens. Psalms 19:10 says it is *"sweeter also than honey and the honeycomb"*.

* **Let it set in your heart until it burns:**
(Luke 24:32) *"And they said one to another; Did not our heart burn within us while he talked with us by the way, and while he opened to us the scriptures?"*

"Get your children's attitude right and the fruit will be right," says Owen.

Becoming a Bayaday Chef

Chef Bayaday uses the term haute cuisine in regard to high end life meals that one creates for family. It means you are cooking with the best ingredients, best quality and the best seasonings. It is said that not all steaks are equal. Why? The cut of meat determines the taste. Use quality ingredients when dealing with your children.

David expresses his confidence in God's design in Psalms 138:8 with his declarative statement of *"concerneth me."* Psalms 138:8 is like Jeremiah 29:11, *"I know the thoughts that I have toward you, saith the Lord, thoughts of peace ..."* Parents can shatter the good in the family with vain thoughts (Jeremiah 4:14). Many family gatherings have no happy ending. Children can reject parents and parents can reject their children. Children can become upset and the parents will become upset. Rejection, being upset or having anger can destroy the fruitfulness of a good life meal.

The meaning of concern in Psalms 138:8 refers to reflectiveness. God is always trying to create fruitfulness in us. Parents should do the same which means taking time, sharing and reflecting with their children. God shows us that he reflects more on what we could be than what we are. Parents need to reflect on the good of the child, not the faults.

Menus that Matter

Chef Bayaday says that he knows of a family that created haute cuisine by moving from a negative to a positive life meal. What they do once a week is quote Jeremiah 29:11 and make it very personal -- *"For I know the thoughts I have toward"* my son, my daughter. As a parent I have thoughts of peace and good.

Spend time with each one of your children and tell them what your thoughts are. Have them tell each of their brothers and sisters and express their thoughts of good toward the parents.

My Menus for Life Meals of Fruitfulness

1. My own menu for creating good thoughts toward my child.

2. The menu for creating good thoughts toward parents.

A Recipe for Doing Stupid - Watchlessness

Have you ever eaten burnt toast? Who hasn't? The great cooks can multi-task by keeping several jobs going and never burning the food.

Paul in II Timothy 4:5 gives the key to preventing burnt toast, *"Watch thou in all things."* To be an effective cook you must keep an "eye on the pot." Judges chapter 11 is the story of a man who failed to keep his eyes on what he was cooking. Jephthah is the man who lives in a continual stage of watchlessness -- a man who does not watch his words, ways or will.

Jephthah interjected his will into a plan so he made a deal with God. He could have said to himself, "I'll sacrifice, thus showing my devotion to you, so help me win because I want to be the leader of Gilead," It is so easy to allow unclear thinking to keep one from praying for help. It is easier to just promise to give something than to think about the promise.

Jephthah's will to win blinded him to one important truth. That truth was, "What is it that God requires?" Some 675 years later it was still the question that Micah asked in Micah 6:7, *"Will the Lord be pleased with thousands of rams, or with ten thousands of rivers of oil? Shall I give my firstborn for my transgression, the fruit of my body for the sin of my soul?"* Real devotion is not the outward giving of your child but the giving of your heart and life.

The phrase "burnt toast" hints to the time in which bread parts were eaten according to one's status. During the 1500's workers received the burnt bottom of a loaf. The family received the middle and guests were given the top, or "upper crust."

Jephthah's story is the failure of creating an atmosphere of "upper crust" which is the best part of the bread. Failing to watch led him to eating not the "upper crust" but burnt toast.

For sixty days he waited and watched J.D.. He failed to watch his ways, words, and will and ended up burning his toast. Jephthah delivered a weapon of destruction to his life by not being watchful. He had been blessed with a family, yet he burned his daughter.

Cooking with J. D.

Jephthah forgot an important thing about cooking. You should watch the heat and not let the toast burn. He is a master at not keeping his eyes on the prize. J.D. on the other hand, had watchfulness about her. Being in a stressful position because of her father, she accepted her life meal with integrity. J.D. no doubt made a covenant in her heart, "I'll be true".

Culturally, J. D.'s life meal is much like Isaac's. It was to be determined by their fathers. Abraham was asked by God to give his son as a sacrifice whereas Jephthah was directed by his own will. A vow from her father was in poor taste because there was no watchfulness.

The emotional side of J. D. hints of Jesus' words of going the second mile. Maintaining her clarity of thought kept her from becoming a party animal during the two months that she spent on the mountain. Today the chaos of sexual identity is bewildering. J. D. could have gone off the deep end and experienced the wild side of life. But she is very watchful of her soul and her integrity. If you want to cook a good life meal be very watchful! The short and long term effects of a life meal can be disastrous.

J. D. was able to keep two things alive in those two months. She had a vital relationship with God to keep herself pure. She kept the relationship pure by watching over her own soul.

God's Recipe for Overcoming Watchlessness

Remember: Watchlessness is a constant state of not being watchful about one's life meal.

* **Take one cup of Children of Light:**

(I Thessalonians 5:5-6) *"children of light" ... v.6 ... "but let us watch and be sober."*

* **One cup of expect the unexpected:**

(Revelation 16:15) *"Behold I come as a thief. Blessed is he that watcheth ..."*

* **One cup of temptation free:**

(Matthew 26:41) *"Watch and pray, that ye enter not into temptation."*

* **One cup of stand fast:**

(I Corinthians 16:13) *"watch ye, stand fast in the faith ..."*

* **One cup of teaching:**

(Matthew 28:20) *"Teaching them to observe all things whatsoever I have commanded."*

* **Mix well and add:**

One cup of Personal Responsibility (remember Jephthah did not use this and did not watch over J. D.)

* **Bake with the fire of the Holy Spirit:**

(I John 2:20) *"But ye have an unction from the Holy One ..."*

Owen says, "Parents sometimes demand unreasonable things, so watch yourself."

Becoming a Bayaday Chef

The understanding of Psalms 138:8 is how the Lord chose to perfect. He will work out His plans for my life for what concerns Him. To work out one's plans takes watchfulness. Judges 11 is the story of Jephthah's failure to watch over his family which caused him to burn his toast.

Chef Bayaday states that in life parents can fail to be watchful. There is a principle in life. No job is so simple that it cannot be done wrong. A parent's way of handling conflict usually becomes the children's way. The words which parents use in life usually become the children's words. A parent's will can negatively affect the child's will, causing them to develop the wrong type of outlook.

Menus that Matter

A great way to include your children in the watchfulness of life is by playing "What is it that I want?" For example, if a child wants a cellphone, have them tell why having a cellphone is important. They should ask the child and then allow him to give an answer. What words and actions would cause me to respond positively to his request? The family must be watchful about their words, ways and will.

My Menus For Life Meals of Watchfulness

1. My own menu that helps to watch over our words.

2. My own menu that helps to watch over our ways.

3. My own menu that helps to watch over our will.

A Recipe for Doing Stupid – Plentilessness

It has been said that women delight in three words -- "I love you." On the other hand, men enjoy hearing four words -- "All you can eat." What is better than a seafood buffet? The experience of a buffet can be exuberant.

Sometimes the exuberance of a buffet can be lost due to what is being served. No doubt Jephthah felt exuberance when he won the battle. His exuberance was his catch of the day, giving him enthusiasm for his victory. However, his buffet becomes a "fish with its head still attached." One has to wonder if the catch of the day still has its eyes. I must confess that I don't care for fish that has been cooked with its head and eyes. But, did Jephthah enjoy fish heads with eyes? Having the privilege to travel I have been served chicken feet, coffee that would put a humming bird into hyper speed and fish heads with eyes. Not all meals make good buffets as Jephthah discovers.

The uniqueness of fishing is the use of lures. Lure means to catch, to ensnare; as a woman who is captivated by the charm of a man. A little over three hundred years before Jephthah, Israel heard that the gods of other nations would be *"as thorns in your sides"* and *"a snare unto you"* (Deuteronomy 7:16).

Jephthah has been lured away from correct living because he has eaten from the wrong buffet. That buffet featured his catch of the day which was his vow. He believed in Yahweh yet he shocks the reader by his decline in his life choices, such as offering his daughter.

His act of godlessness is self-willing much like the lady who went on a cruise. She was looking for "a catch". Standing in a buffet line she smiled at a man. The next day the man walked up and said, "I can't help but notice that you are looking at me." "Why yes, I am! You have a strong resemblance to my third husband." "How many times have you been married?" he asked. With a warm smile she replied "Two." Both examples reveal self-will.

Did Jephthah at any point feel a sense of overwhelming loss? Did anyone ever say, "I don't want to be his friend, for he may want to sacrifice me?" Was there an outcry because of this act? Did his wife even want to be by him again? Did she see him as a loser or a winner? Was his own soul ravished by self-imposed rejection, making him feel the loss of having plenty?

The effect of Jephthah's catch of the day, which was his vow, caused him to become a sad, lonely man (11:35). He no doubt lived where *"all joy"* became *"darkened"* (Isaiah 24:11).

Watch out for the catch of the day! You may be eating fish heads and eye balls, which can cause your exuberance to be turned into sadness.

Cooking with J. D.

Everyone wants a culinary delight--that one special meal that they really enjoy. Travis Phillips says, "I think God created the chicken knowing that P. F. Chang would someday add sesame seeds and create a culinary bliss." For some the culinary bliss would be more in tune with a buffet, which was created for the "Maybes." Maybe I'll have this dish or, maybe I'll try that. Oh No, I'll try it all! In Savannah, Georgia they have Miss Wilkes Dining Room, a place that serves family style meals with 21 different dishes. Quite the experience, with good food and lots of it!

J. D. had to eat her father's life meal, but before she did, she created her own buffet life meal. Her meal of choice is fellowship and companions (Judges 11:37-38). When one has to eat the catch of the day of poor parenting they should have a buffet of emotional help.

Abuse and neglect are not new to this world. The brokenness of this present generation finds roots in parents creating a bad life meal. Many young people today did not choose their meal, but their parents chose it for them.

J. D. is old enough to create her own life meal. Her choice was a buffet that lasted two months and gave her emotional and spiritual help. It became her buffet of worth.

God's Recipe for Overcoming Plentilessness

Remember: Plentilessness is a continual state of a life meal that has no exuberance.

* **Name of Dish - Be careful Dish:**
     You need plenty of good friends that are positive.

* **Add two cups of stickers:**
     Jesus is a friend that sticks closer than a brother.

* **Add one cup of blessing (I Corinthians 10:16).**
     "The cup of blessing which we bless, is it not the communion of the blood of Christ?"

* **Add two cups of partakers of the Lord (I Corinthians 10:21).**
     "Ye cannot drink the cup of the Lord and the cup of devils; ye cannot be partakers of the Lord's Table and the table of devils."

Owen says, "Eating at a buffet can cause you to gain weight, because you always have a tendency to overeat." Make sure your buffet has the right dishes as Jephthah's did not.

Becoming a Bayaday Chef

At times parents and children can feel a sense of shame, and unforgiveness. Psalms 138:8 should help people realize the worth and importance that God instills in them. Low performance and self-rejection leads to one feeling under-valued and a loss of exuberance.

Every parent has a desire to soar in parenting, but many times they feel like they only creep along. Creeping can become the catch of the day. Creeping is a slow moving experience. As parents, we don't want to creep, but to move forward in helping our children experience great life meals.

Menus that Matter

To become a Chef Bayaday you need to create ways to blend both the "catch of the day" and exuberance for life. One can find many meals that become the "catch of the day". Life meals can be of hate or acceptance, of unforgiveness or forgiveness. What parents catch becomes the life meal.

Chef Bayaday tells of a couple who use their love for music to create life meals of worth. Take your children and explain different concepts that are being sung. Have everyone to share a thought for a song. Each family member needs to share a concept of worth about family members, animals, hope, home or love. The list can go on and on. Help each child to express worth in others. Write the song of worth! Let family worth become the "catch of the day" and express it with exuberance.

My Menus For a Life Meal That is Plentiful

1. My own menu for the "catch of the day".

2. My own menu for seeing the positive in people and in God.

A Recipe for Doing Stupid – Centerlessness

The different seasons bring different colors. Those colors are for our benefit so that we can see the creative beauty of nature. Some people enjoy the spring colors whereas others enjoy the fall splashes. Either can be used to make a beautiful centerpiece.

Jephthah's life ended without a centerpiece! There was no adornment on his table that spoke of beauty.

Decor is a style of decorating to enhance a meal. Most men don't see the importance of a centerpiece which is used to brighten the mood of the meal. It enhances the meal as an ornamental object to aid the sense of sight. The food will assault the sense of sight, smell, and taste. The decor of a centerpiece brings color that brightens and warms a room.

Jephthah's vow is not a centerpiece that you would want to be remembered by. He does not center his life with beauty. His life became a centerless centerpiece.

The Bible says in Judges 11:2 that they thrust him out. The term "thrust" means to be driven out or to be banished from both family and society. Such an experience could lead one to believe that he was probably called names, criticized by his stepmother, and made fun of by his brothers. All of these experiences probably left him building dark thoughts. Life had crushed him and he probably felt all alone.

With no thought of his vow, he vowed with the dark thoughts still in his soul. He believed in God but his nature was still the same -- the kid who had been left all alone.

No one helped Jephthah to move beyond his dark thoughts or helped him to realize that life, love, and accomplishments, give color to life's centerpiece. His most tragic moment occurred when he felt that it was "no big deal" to take someone's life.

He ate at a table that had no centerpiece. His table was centerless. Jephthah failed his soul and it became a soul of leanness, not allowing God to be his centerpiece (Psalms 106:15). He failed to see the beauty of his God, the giver of life.

As parents we must ask ourselves; "What is the centerpiece in my life?" "Does it add to my children's lives, or does it take away from their lives?"

The centerpiece in your soul should be honoring your children in a Godly way and not provoking them to wrath. Verbal abuse or an atmosphere of fear never honors God. Watch what your centerpiece is!

Cooking with J. D.

J. D. had to receive a life meal that had no decor. Decor is that outward part of a meal. Centerpiece, place mats, pictures, paint or wallpaper set the stage for a meal. Colors and brightness aid in a good tasting meal.

Jephthah did cook a life meal that would be tasteless. It was a meal without color or cheeriness and one that was sad. So what does J. D. do? She creates a decor from within -- the inner decor of her soul. Here is where many people fail. They don't, or can't, bring color into life meals. Everyone in the world is their own interior designer.

As an interior designer we have the responsibility to maintain decor and give color to both our impression and reality of life. J. D. celebrates life for two months. This becomes her moment for deciding her own decor. Can she, as she bewails her virginity, also create a centerpiece for her life meal?

Creating a centerpiece takes time -- finding flowers, leaves, rocks, etc. all become a personal creation. But the centerpiece of a life meal is harder to see. In two months of crying she submits in that she *"returned unto her father"* (Judges 11:39).

Most people would run away instead of returning. Her life meal was that she gave her word and kept it. It is here in the integrity of her words, that we find her center that becomes her centerpiece.

God's Recipe for Overcoming No Center

Remember: Put Christ as the centerpiece in life meals.

* **What is the core center?**
Take one cup of "set."
(I Chronicles 29:3) *"I have set my affection to the house of my God ..."*

* **Add two cups of "object for life."**
(Philippians 3:13) *"This one thing I do, forgetting those things which are behind, and reaching forth unto those things which are before"*

* **Mix in two tablespoons of "chosen."**
(Joshua 24:15) *Choose you this day whom ye will serve.*
    - Choose devotion to God over the transient pleasures.
    - Choose devotion to God over temporal interests.

* **Bake in the heart for one hour:**
    - Cover your core center with the ingredients of a settled purpose.

- A settled purpose - *"He must needs go through Samaria"* (John 4:4).

Owen says, "My centerpiece in life is to be positive and pray."

Becoming a Bayaday Chef

When the Bible says the Lord *"will perfect that which concerneth me"* (Psalms 138:8), it is like adding a beautiful centerpiece to the table. Centerpieces can create the mood for a life meal. The concern that God has for you is the same concern that a parent should have for their children.

Psalms 138:8 gives the intent and the desired end that guides, helps, protects, establishes and encourages. This is what parents should do for their children.

Chef Bayaday says that parents can create beautiful centerpieces, or they can create a centerpiece that reveals the ugliness of rejection. A beautiful centerpiece shows the beauty of Christ. In the song "Battle Hymn of the Republic" there is a line that says, "In the beauty of the lilies, Christ was born across the sea, with a glory in his bosom that transfigures you and me." Christ is a centerpiece of love that transforms us.

The centerpiece of the beauty of Christ can be an agent of change. Chef Bayaday says it takes a lot of energy to create transforming moments. One way to do this is by teaching children not to make fun or judge other people. Some people think they are better, others think they are not good enough. They may think they are not good looking enough and not smart enough. Children who live this way usually find themselves lacking in the ability to manage their lives well.

Menus that Matter

Chef Bayaday tells of a young man who came to learn the value of his dad's life. He watched his dad helping other people, and when his dad died he began to realize his Dad's lasting influence. That influence was not with money or education! After the funeral this young man for the next 35 years used his dad's example of positive influence to create a beautiful centerpiece that aided life's meals.

Chef Bayaday says that this dad influences his son. Together they have had over 120 years of positive centerpieces. Those years center on Acts 10:38, *"who went about doing good."*

My Menus for Life Meals of Creating a Centerpiece

1. My own menu for making the beauty of Christ known to my children.

2. My own menu for making the beauty of Christ known to others.

Recipe for Doing Stupid – Partylessness

A gala for Jephthah --he won the war! Now was the time to recognize his accomplishments and contributions to the war effort. Captains, advisors and men of valor would be part of the evening. There was going to be a great celebration. There would be a gala in Gilead.

The event was probably on everyone's mind as they marched towards home. The gala would center on a theme, and young girls would dance while the young men would try to hear the latest story of war.

As the old philosopher, Fred Flintstone says, "You'll have a yabba-dabba-doo time. A dabba doo time. You'll have a gay old time."   But, when it was almost time for celebrating, there arose a roadblock to the gala. Their achievements are about to be overshadowed. Victory accomplishments ring hollow when it is understood what Jephthah has done.

Events collide when a daughter walks out the front door and runs headlong into a vow. I wish there could be a re-do button. We all sometimes need a "redo" in life, but a promise is a promise.

Jephthah receives new education! He discovers that his devotional faith could be buried under layers of hardness and harshness, producing a soul that has become partyless.   His constant state of cynicism in life moves him into a reactionary depression -- a life of no party.

In this partylessness of soul Jephthah moves into a joyless worship. Being a Pastor for thirty-five years, I have seen people full of devotion and enjoying their worship experience.

However, under life's pressures devotion can lose its zeal and the worship implodes. The main focus in worship is never intellectual, but finding peace in the soul. The beauty of worship happens in the soul when a person finds peace. Peace helps to unwind a troubled mind.

Did Jephthah ever feel any remorse about what he had done? The victory of war lost its appeal, hindering progress. Why did he fail with his family? John MacArthur gives some reasons that show Jephthah's failure in vow making. He lived beyond the Jordan, far from the tabernacle, a hypocrite in religious devotion. He was familiar with human sacrifice among other nations and was influenced by such superstition. He wanted victory badly. Even though he was influenced by the human sacrifices, he probably meant a burnt offering. Unfortunately, it was his daughter.

Jephthah's gala turned into a sad, bizarre thing. His vow is inconsistent with the ways of God and one's devotion toward God.

Dads beware of what your Gala Celebration could turn into!

Cooking with J. D.

Galas are special social gatherings for conversation, refreshment and enjoyment. Jephthah's gala was the one where he became his own party pooper. His vow would drain the spirit of the victory party.

J. D.'s gala was two months with her friends. Her time with her friends probably allowed her to handle her emotions. No doubt they were always changing emotions ranging from highs to deep lows. But the story of Judges, chapter 11 allows one to see a positive attitude.

Did her friends express to her their feelings about their fathers? A friend of hers may have expressed what she liked or disliked about family. No doubt she would listen to her friends talking and remember her own memories. In moments of sad life meals that have to be eaten, one can find memories of better times. J. D.'s gala must have been a different experience!

True to fashion, J. D. made improvements to her own life. She was remembered and that became her gala. She was remembered as innocent and good. Have you ever eaten in a bad restaurant? You will remember the experience and not go there again. A good experience in a good restaurant makes you want to go back. Everyone remembered Jephthah's gala as bad, and J. D.'s gala of a young girl who was faithful to her place in life.

God's Recipe for Overcoming a Bad Gala

Remember: A soul that eats life meals of negativity creates poor galas.

* Confidence Cake:
- One cup of "brought me up."
- (Psalms 40:2) *"He brought me up out of a horrible pit."*
- Life pits - fear, despair, loneliness.

* Use two cups of "set"
- (Psalms 40:2) *"set my feet upon a rock."*

* Mix well:
- Add two tablespoons of keep me going
- (Psalms 40:2) *"established my goings."*
- Mix in 8 ounces of "a new song"
- (Psalms 40:3) *"put a new song in my mouth, even praise unto our God."*

Owen says, "A bad life meal is a bad gala."

Becoming a Bayaday Chef

God has a concern for all. The concept of concern is determination. God has great determination to save people. He knows what the destiny of people should be. Jesus gives the heart of his desire when he says he wants us to have life abundantly (John 10:10) or a party.

Parties can be fun and enjoyable. They add positive moments of socialization. A good party helps the mind to feel acceptance. That is the beauty of the marriage supper of the Lamb.

Jephthah's gala should be a festive time. But it turns into an unprofitable moment of sadness.

Menus that Matter

Chef Bayaday says that celebrations that end well are the best galas. Jephthah's gala does not end well. So how can a parent create times of gala in their children's life?

Every time the family feels they have been blessed by God they should have a celebration. It may be a missed accident or an answered prayer. It may be a performance or doing a Bible reading. Anything that the family feels is a spiritual victory can turn into a celebration. It may be a popcorn celebration or an ice cream and cake celebration. One may want to have a favorite meal celebration. The key is to celebrate when one has victory.

My Menu for a Life Meal of Partying

1. My own menu for a celebration for the family dealing with victory.

2. My own menu for a celebration for the little victories of faith or courage.

A Recipe for Doing Stupid – Flavorlessness

In cooking you can take ingredients and cook them slowly, reducing the substance into a sticky soup or into a savory sauce. Good sauces that have good ingredients produce the best flavor. I myself am not a cook but I am a person who enjoys good tasting food, and I have learned that sometimes the cheaper ingredients do not produce the desired taste.

When it comes to life Jephthah does not seek the best. He wants a succulent flavor but he takes rejection and reduces it to a flavorless reduction. For the next seventy-four months Jephthah experiences the pain of disrespecting his daughter's life. It does not produce a great tasting sauce.

It's easy to cook a reduction sauce, but the issue is the taste. Jephthah cooked a reduction that had no flavor because he suffered from "instant-speak" reflex. David Taylor calls Jephthah the "Old Testament Peter" -- speaking when he should not (Matthew 17:4). Instant speak reflex happens when you say, "You are so stupid," or "I told you ten times to stop that. Can't you ever do anything right?" Such negative outbursts can easily provoke children to anger (Ephesians 6:4). Writer, Nancy Kline, states, "To take time to think is to gain time to live." (Bits & Pieces). One needs to stop and think of the dangers in rash vows of devotion or unchecked words.

Blurting out words can sometimes lead to regret and frustration. In the past had Jephthah ever made rash statements? He probably had. It is a very easy habit-forming thing to do. Was there ever anyone who had told him, "You need to be careful?" One time my wife told me, "You just about lost your son" because of a rash demand that I had made. It is very easy to provoke or anger someone so that they are "enraged by words."

To guard your heart so that one does not use rash words takes a lot of grace. The book of James, chapter 3, talks about the untamable tongue. He states that the unwise tongue can defile the body, set on fire our natural life, and cause us to experience a hellish moment (James 3:6).

Sauces made from reductions are naturally thick, hearty and redolent with flavor and have a pleasant, fragrant odor. Owen Austin adds flavor to the lives of others by being able to give positive input. He gives flavor that is tasteful.

Cooking with J. D.

Life sometimes loses its flavor during a crisis. Jephthah's crisis was self-imposed and caused chaos in the family. He won a hard victory over the enemy, but did not win over himself. His life had become a reduction of a flavorless sauce. His psychological loss happened because he cooked a very poor, plain life meal.

A reduction is made to enhance a meal. But a reducation should not overpower the meal. So, J. D. created flavor in her life meal by not overpowering her mouth. Jephthah's mouth overpowered his ability to create a good life meal because of his vow. Remember Dennis the Menace? His family has a look of horror when, while they are eating, Dennis says, "I didn't want your food to get cold, so I put some very hot sauce on it." Jephthah's vow became the hot sauce that destroyed J. D.'s life.

J. D.'s psychological makeup is probably different than her fathers. It seems that God allows "his vanity to run its course." (Sandy Shapoval, p11). J. D.'s course provides a different look. She accepts the life meal, being obedient and maintaining her purity. Together they created her reduction. Her life meal had flavor.

God's Recipe for Overcoming Flavorlessness

Remember: It takes the best ingredients to create the best flavor.

* A recipe for spiritual discernment:

Two cups of discerning taste--Jephthah had no discernment

(Job 6:30) *"Is there iniquity in my tongue? Cannot my taste discern perverse things?"*

* Mix in one teaspoon of salt (adds savor to life's meal.):

Salt is the purifying agent of the Gospel in our lives.

(Job 6:6) *"Can that which is unsavory be eaten without salt? or is there any taste in the white of an egg?"*

* Four cups of goodness:

- Goodness of salvation. (Romans 2:4)
- Goodness in help. (Nahum 1:7)
- Goodness of righteousness. (Psalms 33:5)
- Good teacher. (Psalms 25:8)

* Best to eat every day:

- (Psalms 34:8) *"O taste and see that the Lord is good."*

Owen says, "God has been very good to me all these 93 years, and that goodness has flavored my life."

Becoming a Bayaday Chef

Jephthah found out what could happen in life for six years. After his vow was completed there was sadness. Sadness in the heart will leave a bad tasting reduction. Because Jephthah failed to reduce his sauce that he had created the sauce did not have a good flavor.

Because Jephthah failed to provide the right ingredients, his sauce became a flavorless life meal. Psalms 138:8 is God facilitating our life. He wants to guide all parents so that they are engaged in a faith building family that experiences faith. A parent's faith should contain the right ingredients so that the children can understand what faith is and how to apply it to their lives.

Menus that Matter

Chef Bayaday says that it is easy to be a pathetic parent. Jephthah becomes pathetic by using his heart to reduce the wrong ingredients. He tells of a family that had a newspaper prayer. They read the paper! One family's home burns down and they say a prayer for the people. Then they try to do something positive for the family that lost their home. The aim is to help children experience a good sauce for their lives.

My Menu for Life Meals of Flavor

1. My own menu that adds flavor to my children.

2. My own menu that adds flavor to my friends.

A Recipe for Doing Stupid – Tastelessness

The French use words that have made themselves a part of the cooking/eating experience. One such word is â la carte. It deals with how a dish is prepared -- manner and taste. Ă la carte is the ability to order a dish by itself. One has the right to pick and choose. Jephthah's right to choice was "Rex-lēx" (Latin for king rules or king over the law). This warrior/leader now believes this is his right.

Who does not remember the Indiana Jones movie, *The Last Crusade*? There is a point in the movie where the Grail Knight states, "You have to choose the grail." Donovan chooses to drink from a cup and he turns into dust. The Grail Knight declares, "He chose poorly." Such a line can be used for Jephthah. He chose poorly. His â la carte was a "Rex-lēx meal." In all honesty, Judges is really about Judges and society choosing poorly.

The single dish Jephthah should have chosen was lēx-rex or law over the king. Two philosophers, Nietzsche and Machiavelli, drive home this concept of power as the makeup of men. It is a quest for power or to be a ruler.

The drive to be in control is much like Pepe Le Pew, the French skunk. He always chased the female cats that somehow ended up with a white stripe down the middle of their back. True to form, Pepe always fell head over heels in love and set out to win the "cats". But, poor old Pepe Le Pew never caught a girlfriend. Why? He deceived himself by thinking every black animal with a white stripe was a skunk.

This is what Jephthah did. He deceives himself believing his â la carte is his best choice. In trying to make a deal with God for victory, he vows a vow. He is willing to sacrifice the first thing that comes out of the door (Judges 11:31). He is Rex-lēx (above the law or no law to restrain his choice). Does the choice of his vow ever leave him with a good conscience? A good clear conscience happens in the pursuit of what is morally right. David's sin is ever before him (Psalms 51:3) not having a clear conscience. Jephthah's action would always be before him.

Cooking with J. D.

One word can be used to describe Jephthah's dish of choice -- "waste." Jackie Kennedy said, "If I hadn't married you (J.F.K.) my life would have been tragic, because the definition of tragic is a waste." (O'Rielly. 223) Jephthah's â la carte life meal becomes a wasted tragedy. It is a flavorless meal that would be rejected 3,500 years by society.

J. D. needs an â la carte of grace. Today modern men experience grace in Jesus. But J. D. needs her father to extend grace and it never comes. Can someone say something, or do something that would help her? Can her father cook a better life meal? Can he find a different answer to his vow? Can he not redeem his vow? (Leviticus 27:2-3). The passage does not hint that he even tried to undo the vow. J. D. will have to eat this poor life meal and it will become a waste. Wasted life meals are never family favorites.

No doubt J. D. wanted the flavor of Psalms 127:3, *"Lo, children are an heritage of the Lord: and the fruit of the womb is his reward."* Such will not be her life! What will add flavor? Being obedient, she steadfastly *"returned unto her father, who did with her according to his vow:"* (Judges 11:39)

Today women face numerous challenges, but many seem to rise up in steadfastness and keep their integrity. Did J. D. hear of Ruth's steadfastness in following Naomi (Ruth 1:18) and say this will be my â la carte?

God's Recipe for Overcoming Tastelessness

Remember: The best â la carte life meals are tasteful.

* **One cup of awareness:**

(Lamentations 3:22) *"It is of the Lord's mercies that we are not consumed, because his   compassions fail not."*

* **Add one teaspoon of good:**

(Proverbs 11:17) *"The merciful man doeth good to his own soul:"*

* **Add one teaspoon doing:**

(Hebrews 2:3) *"How shall we escape, if we neglect so great salvation ..."*

* **Add one teaspoon of warning against fear:**

(Matthew 25:25) *"And I was afraid and went and hid thy talent in the earth ..."*

* **Add two teaspoons of thorn killer so the Word can grow:**

(Mathew. 13:22) *"He also that received seed among the thorns is he that heareth the word; and the care of this world, and the deceitfulness of riches, choke the word, and he becometh unfruitful."*

* **Mix well and add two cups of oil of the wise—wise people don't want waste:**

(Proverbs 21:20) *"There is treasure to be desired and oil in the dwelling of the wise."*

Owen says, "I wasted so many good years before I knew the Lord."

Becoming a Bayaday Chef

Everyone wants the right to choose a meal. Usually one's choice is based on taste. There are taste buds on the tongue that allow a person the experience of enjoyment. Jephthah's vow was his taste of joy before his daughter made her appearance. But, once she arrived he probably was never allowed to taste joy again.

When one chooses a meal based on personal taste they can have an ă la carte. Psalms 138:8 is David saying that God has a perfect ă la carte for you. He has great concern for you because he knows your tastes.

The Bible has many dishes that are ă la carte. Proverbs 3:5-6 is an ă la carte for personal guidance. Revelation 3:15 is a dish for personal fellowship. If you have peace or want peace, enjoy a meal of John 14:1-2. You can have an ă la carte spiritual meal by reading the Bible and allowing a particular verse to "speak" to you.

Menus that Matter

Chef Bayaday tells of a family that creates life meals based on the children's taste. How is it that one can develop a taste or love for something? You must try something to see if you have a love or a taste for it.

Have each child tell what they enjoy doing. Then try to expand the activity into a spiritual side. A child may enjoy a sport. Allow the child to teach others who are younger. Help the child to explain a spiritual truth when teaching the sport.

It is rewarding to share an activity with others. It is very fulfilling to share truth; therefore, combine activity with truth. Life meals have to taste good or children will not eat them.

My Menu for a Life Meal of Taste

1. My own menu that tries different things that teaches ă la carte of spiritual truth.

2. My own menu that allows children to develop a new sense of taste.

A Recipe for Doing Stupid – Marinatelessness

Who does not like tender meat? Marinating a steak adds to its flavor and tenderness. Marinade is a multi-million dollar business in America. Why? It adds so much to the taste and tenderness of meat.

When it comes to life, people want pizzazz -- a dynamic zest in their life. There is a French term called, "je ne sais quor" or, "I know not what." Everyone wants zest in life even if they do not know what produces it.

Jephthah is looking for pizzazz -- to win in style and be flashy. In an attempt to ensure his chance of winning he makes a vow. To understand the story of Jephthah you have to realize that he never considered if his vow was tender or tough. With a personal desire to win, Jephthah tries to make a deal with God. Was he affected by a cause and effect and his relationship to God? First, his religious understanding of God fails to reach a level where he knew God out of holiness in a personal, powerful way. Next, he seems to be impacted by his culture. His devotion was not from his heart with a loving attitude toward others. It was by his actions "that became harsh and tough" says Owen Austin. Lastly, Jephthah's vow is of his own creation. It is what he wants to do, even if he doesn't know the end result of his vow.

The reason that Jephthah made a vow may not be truly known, but what is known is that 675 years later Micah asks what God requires? (Micah 6:8) Did Jephthah think his vow was what God required rather than to "do justly" and "walk humbly" with God?

As a warrior/leader who wanted acceptance, he was lured away from clear thinking. His thinking had been affected by the practices of his time, which causes him to take on a worldly mind-set. (James 3:13-18)

With no confident anticipation of trusting in God's help he becomes much like an alcoholic. He is a person with an alcoholic fog in his mind, believing that his self-imposed vow puts pizzazz in life.

Jephthah's marinade is his own creation. What he forgets is an important ingredient-- salt! Seasoning in the right amount adds zest to the marinade. Jephthah never seasoned his speech in the right way to create an enjoyable dish. Every steak from this day forward will be just food without pizzazz or zest. His life will come to a place where all joy becomes darkness.

Cooking with J. D.

Pizzaz is a zest for life, which is what many want. J. D. would try to create pizzazz in life. How? One can only wonder! How does one go about fixing a life meal that has pizzazz or meaning?

To have great zest in life one must accent a positive life meal. Jephthah, with his personal demon of rejection, cuts life, dreams and family short. J. D. has moved into independence by asking for two months.

So here are the facts! Jephthah tries to have pizzazz in his life and receives only unhappiness. J. D. discovers self-awareness for two months. She is in charge of her personal style. By being obedient, she finds significance in her life.

If one could interview J. D. today the question to ask her would be, "What best life meal would you fix?" She might say, "Add pizzazz to life by realizing that your words need to be marinated with grace." She definitely would say, "Never marinate like my dad with his rash vow."

God's Recipe for Overcoming no Marinade
Remember: Allow the Word of God to always marinade the heart so there is pizzazz.

* **One teaspoon of not being rash:**
    (Ecclesiastes 5:2) *"Be not rash with thy mouth and let not thine heart be hasty to utter anything before God."*

* **One teaspoon of realizing labor is vanity:**
    (Ecclesiastes 1:14) *"I have seen all the works that are done under the sun: and, behold, all is vanity and vexation of Spirit."*

* **One tablespoon of realizing worldly wisdom is sorrow:**
    (Ecclesiastes 1:18) *"he that increaseth knowledge increaseth sorrow."*

* **Two cups of remember:**
    (Ecclesiastes 12:1) *"Remember now thy Creator."*

* **Three cups of sobering certainties:**
    (Ecclesiastes 12:14) *"For God shall bring every work into judgment."*

* **Mix well and add three cups of conclusion:**
    (Ecclesiastes 12:13) *"Let us hear the conclusion of the whole matter: Fear God, and keep his commandments: for this is the whole duty of man."*

* **Add a pinch of salt.**
    (Matthew 5:13) *"ye are the salt of the earth ....."*

Owen says, "Her soul shines in her dark life meal."

Becoming a Bayaday Chef

If you want to cook life meals that add pizzazz to life then you have to learn how to help others. Jephthah wants pizzazz for his family but ends up oppressive.

To be a Great Bayaday Chef you have to show concern for what is oppressive to people. Life is a struggle. Some families will not survive. The struggle for a safe home is a home that enables children to feel safe without chaos.

Pizzazz comes from being tender. A tender steak means it is not tough. A tender minded person is compassionate. The Bayaday Chef is taking Psalms 138:8, and with concern shows tenderness. Tenderness comes from the marinade that one uses. Always use the marinade of grace with your words.

Menus that Matter

Chef Bayaday has a family that uses tenderness as a game. Parents need to do this with each other. The wife and the husband both have the right to express to their mate the lack of tenderness. They may be rough and tough with words and actions. These words or actions can be picked up by the children. When someone in the family becomes "rough" with their words, have them stop and think how they could say or do it differently. Everyone has times when they say or do things they shouldn't to others. Remember that tenderness brings pizzazz to life!

My Menu for a Life Meal With Pizzazz

1. My own menu that formulates pizzazz and tenderness for my mate.

3. My own menu that creates connections of tenderness for my children.

Cuisine Conclusion

Meals are a part of the fabric of every culture. The cuisine of each culture reveals that country's tastes. China has a particular style of cooking and Mexico has another. Experiencing different types of cuisine allows people to determine if they enjoy one or the other. Preparing a life meal for your children as their parent may be different from another parent, but just be sure to include good quality Godly ingredients that will be pleasing to their tastes and nourish their souls.

When it comes to life meals, Jephthah's cuisine was characterized by using poor judgment and self-will. He was a taker, not a giver. He took by failing to give his daughter a fruitful and long life.

J.D., on the other hand, immersed herself in Biblical truths and remained true. The principles of submission, honor and respect became her cuisine.

Today, parents who want to cook great life meals that become cuisine delights need to remember four things. First, recall the teachings on how to build strong families. Then reaffirm the rare gift of love you can give and show in a busy world. Next, reflect on life's lessons with your children. Lastly, renew the commitment to be the best parent you can be. These are the things that aid parents when they become overwhelmed and begin to cook a life meal like Jephthah's. Parents, find the Godly cuisine that God has planned for your children's life meal. Then do what Chef Bobby Flay says, "So to all you cooks out there, keep doing what you do!" Go and become the best chef you can for your children.

Made in the USA
San Bernardino, CA
08 August 2014